TONY BUZAN

BRILLIANT MEMORY

Other Tony Buzan titles published by BBC Active:

Buzan Bites
Mind Mapping
Speed Reading

The Mind Set
Use Your Head
Use Your Memory
Master Your Memory
The Speed Reading Book
The Mind Map® Book
The Illustrated Mind Map® Book

Embracing Change

TONY BUZAN

BRILLIANT MEMORY

BBC Active, an imprint of Educational Publishers LLP, part of the Pearson Education Group, Edinburgh Gate, Harlow, Essex, CM20 2JE, England

First published in 2006 by BBC Active
Reprinted 2007

ISBN: 978-0-5635-2033-7

Commissioning Editor: Emma Shackleton
Project Editors: Sarah Sutton and Helena Caldon
Text Designer: Annette Peppis
Cover Designer: R&D&Co Design Ltd
Senior Production Controller: Man Fai Lau
Illustrations by Alan Burton, Lorraine Gill and Nick Buchanan
Printed and bound in China CTPSC/02

The Publisher's policy is to use paper manufactured from sustainable forests.

CONTENTS

Introduction

⊙ How do you rate your memory? Is it good or bad?

⊙ Are you good at remembering some things and not others?

⊙ How are you on: Facts? Faces? Birthdays?

⊙ Do you believe your memory is getting worse as you get older?

⊙ Are you worried about recalling information under pressure at work or in an exam?

⊙ Would you like to be able to remember anything to which you put your mind ?

This handy book provides you with easy-to-follow techniques and explanations of how to develop a supercharged memory that will help to make memory problems and poor information retention a thing of the past. Drawing on the techniques explained in more depth in my books *Use Your Memory* and *Master Your Memory*, I have created this book for time-starved people on the move, who want straightforward routes to increase their memory power.

The good news is that there is no such thing as a naturally 'bad' memory, and that you have the ability to remember as much – or as little – as you want to. Throughout this book I will give you bite-sized pieces of information to help you to understand, improve and enhance your memory. You will learn practical techniques and exercises that will work *with* your brain, so that your memory begins to function more quickly, more effectively and more efficiently than ever before.

Like many children, I was fascinated by the concept of memory when I was a young boy. It amazed me that although I couldn't see it and I didn't know what it looked like, I knew my memory worked and that it was always there. I was bemused that, on the one hand, my memory would operate so efficiently and effectively that I was hardly aware of my thoughts; while on the other hand, especially at school or in exams when I needed to recall precise facts, it seemed to 'fail' me.

As I got older I became more fascinated by memory, and committed myself to developing ways to enhance and improve my memory pathways in order to make optimum use of that amazing part of our anatomy, the brain. This led me to develop my Mind Map® technique, which is now used around the world. (There is a separate *Buzan Bites* book that will tell you about this special memory enhancement method.) Even now, after working in the field for over 30 years, I am amazed at what the mind and memory can do – and how much untapped potential we each have.

It is an exciting prospect to be a part of the research into brain and memory function that is going on around the world at this very moment. The twenty-first century has been called 'The Century of the Brain', and we have entered an extremely invigorating time of discovery and cerebral awakening.

Your memory and your memories are unique to you because no-one else can experience life as you see it and feel it. Only you know how you experience the world and only you can choose how and when to recall past experiences. You may find that you can recall some memories as 'clear as crystal', whereas others seem as cloudy as muddy water or as elusive as a butterfly on the wing. But by the time you have finished reading this book, you will be able to remember everything you wish to with stunning clarity, because you will have the tools to use your mind and memory more efficiently and powerfully than ever before.

Enjoy what will be a memorable experience!

Tony Buzan

1 YOUR AMAZING BRAIN

Your brain is complex, powerful, infinitely variable and astonishing. It never stops working, and it is evolving constantly.

DID YOU KNOW?

◉ In each human brain there are an estimated 1,000,000,000,000 brain cells (also called neurons): that's 1 million, million.

◉ Each individual brain cell is capable of 10,000,000,000,000,000, 000,000,000,000 different connections.

◉ Each individual brain cell is capable of connecting with as many as 10,000 other brain cells at the same instant.

◉ The total number of unique combinations of all the different thoughts available through your brain cell connections, if written down, would amount to a number so large that it would have 10.5 *million kilometres* of noughts after it.

So what does all this mean? It means that the brain is a highly complex and immensely flexible information receiver and transmitter, with a capacity to remember and recall information that is greater than any computer yet invented. Your memory is a part of this highly complex and super-efficient system.

Each brain cell has tens or hundreds or thousands of tentacles called dendrites. These dendrites connect brain cells to each other in order to transmit information via the brain and spinal cord to every part of your body. Every thought, feeling, sensation, taste, instruction or memory is transmitted faster than a speeding bullet. This information radiates from a central point, sending out a series of connecting sparks of data that trigger immediate associations in your brain, and which create information pathways that strengthen every time you repeat the experience.

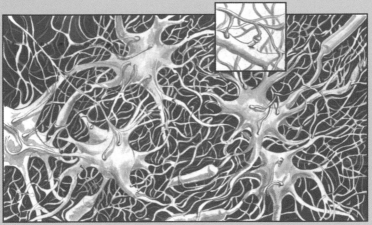

Each thought you have, every sensation you experience, will strengthen or modify previous associations: creating what we know as our memory. Unlike a computer, which has memory banks that eventually 'fill up'; the good news is that your brain's capacity will never fill. The more you learn, the easier it becomes to learn still more.

Fulfil your potential

From the moment your brain begins to develop, and throughout life, you are learning: every moment of every day involves taking in information and adjusting what you know to take account of the new data. Knowledge of *how* the brain works is still in its early stages.

> **DID YOU KNOW?**
> ⊙ Mankind has known where the brain is for only
> 500 years. Before that time it was commonly assumed
> that we thought and felt using the stomach and
> heart – because that is where we experience most
> physical sensation.
> ⊙ Only in the last 20 years have we begun truly to
> understand what the brain does and how it works.

Our relative lack of understanding about how the mind works
has resulted in our using very little of the vast potential
provided by the brain and memory. The sum total of what we use
today is no more that one per cent of what there is to use!

It is highly unlikely that when you were at school you
were taught anything about how your memory functions, how
to use memory techniques, the nature of concentration, of
thinking, motivation or creativity. The memory techniques in
the chapters that follow will show you how you can improve your
performance and increase your potential by enhancing the way
your brain takes in and remembers information.

Your two brains

Information is taken in by your brain and stored in your
memory in many different ways and is processed by either:

⊙ *The right side of the brain* – concerned with: rhythm,
imagination, daydreaming, colour, dimension, spatial awareness,
completeness.

⊙ *The left side of the brain* – concerned with: logic, words, lists,
numbers, sequence, lines, analysis.

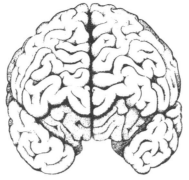

right   **left**

The two sides of your brain do not operate separately from one another – they need to work together to be at their most effective. The more you can stimulate *both sides* of your brain *at the same time*, the more effectively they will work together to help you to:

- ⊙ think better
- ⊙ remember more, and
- ⊙ recall instantly.

The memory systems described in this book are designed to work *with* your brain, not against it; to stimulate your senses and to help your memory to store the information you choose to feed it in an ordered and easily accessible fashion.

> **Get ready to use five super-powered memory systems that will supercharge your brain. In Chapter 2 you will learn how to remember and recall information. Chapter 3 introduces Core Memory Principles to maximize your brainpower. Chapter 4 will unlock your memory, using Key Words and Images; you can then apply all these principles while learning the extraordinary Key Memory Systems described in Chapter 5.**

Helping your brain to learn

A memory system works rather like a super-sized filing cabinet that contains files on every aspect of your entire life. The only way you are going to find information quickly and easily in your cabinet is to make sure that it is well-organized and accessible, so that no matter how obscure the memory you want to retrieve, you know what its category is and can find it and recognize it easily.

In order to be able to categorize and store the information in the filing cabinet that is your memory, it is important to have some understanding of how your brain and memory function while you are learning.

Research has shown that first impressions and last impressions matter to your brain. In every situation, we are more likely to remember things that happen or that are introduced:

- *At the beginning* – the Primacy Effect.
- *At the end* – the Recency Effect.

We also find it easier to remember things that are:

- **Associated** with items or thoughts that are already stored in the memory.
- **Outstanding** or unique – as this appeals to the imagination.

Your brain is more likely to notice and recall something that has strong appeal:

- To your senses: taste, smell, touch, sound or sight.
- To your particular interests.

For a fuller explanation of the reasons for this, see the diagrams and text on page 23–8.

Your brain is geared to create patterns and maps, and to finish sequences; which is why, if a familiar song on the radio stops halfway through, you will probably keep humming it to completion; or if a sequence of paragraphs is numbered one to six and point three is missing, you will search for the missing point three.

Your brain also needs help to remember facts, figures, formulae and other important reference information that needs to be bought quickly to mind. An aid that assists memory is a *mnemonic*.

Although the word will not crop up very often in the course of the book, all the techniques you are about to learn are mnemonic techniques. They are fabulous and effective devices for making optimum use of your mind's capacity to remember anything and everything you choose.

Mnemonics (pronounced 'nem-*on*-ics')

A 'mnemonic' is the name given to a memory aid that helps you to remember something. It may be a word, a picture, a system or other device, that will help you to recall a phrase, a name or a sequence of facts. The 'm' in *mnemonic* is silent and the word comes from the Greek word *mnemon*, which means 'mindful'.

Most of us will have used mnemonic techniques during our schooldays, even if we didn't realize it at the time. Students learning music are often taught the phrase Every Good Boy Deserves Favour to help them remember the notes EGBDF.

If the initial letters were to form a word, the mnemonic would be known as an acronym (*ac*-ro-nim). An acronym is a word that is formed from the first letters of each word, for example: UNESCO, which stands for the United Nations Educational, Scientific and Cultural Organization.

Many of us will have learned the poem *'Thirty days hath September, April, June and November ...'* to help remember which months have 30 days and which have 31 *('except for February, alone ...')*. That too is a mnemonic: a device to help you to remember.

Mnemonics work by stimulating your imagination, and by using words and other tools to encourage your brain to make associations.

I will now introduce you to your perfect memory – and help you to learn how you can start to use it more effectively.

2 YOUR PERFECT MEMORY

Your memory is amazing

Throughout your life you are gathering and storing information that will help you to survive, communicate, learn and form human relationships. Your brain's memory enables you to accumulate knowledge, achieve great things, excel at sport and recognize your friends, enemies and loved ones. Without our memory and our memories we become less than ourselves, and disconnected from the wholeness of life.

There are many misconceptions surrounding memory and memory loss:

⊙ As people get older, they often think that their memories are fading. *This is false thinking,* as I will explain.

⊙ Those who are working under stress may find recalling information a challenge and feel they will never be able to hold anything in their minds for long ever again. However, this is more to do with not giving yourself *time to pause and think*, and having poor methods of recall.

There is one important step to take before doing any further work to superpower your memory: you must *replace any negative thoughts* you might have about your memory being 'bad' with new positive appreciation for the amazing, highly-charged brain you have been given.

⊙ Your memory has more information stored now than it has ever had in your life. There is nothing 'bad' about it, or you.

Over the years you have absorbed a wealth of information: decades-worth of actions, plans, recollections, facts, people, experiences, birthdays, shopping lists, responsibilities and so on.

⊙ Your memory is highly effective – although your process of recalling information may not be as effective as you'd like it to be.

You need only to refine the way you access the information that is stored in your brain.

Remind yourself of some of the extraordinary things your memory can recall without a moment's hesitation:

- The faces of your loved ones.
- How to brush your teeth.
- Your birthday.
- The route from your front door to your office or local shops.
- How to walk.
- How to speak.
- The location of hundreds of different products in all the different shops you patronage.
- Your telephone number.
- Your car registration number.
- Your favourite team's score in the last match.
- Where you were when you were listening to the news on 11 September 2001 (9/11).
- The details of your last holiday.

Each of these thoughts is a very precise memory that involves your brain's dendrites and neurons in a great deal of activity. You know so much, but you probably have never been taught how to manage your mind, or your memory. The systems in this book are your first step to changing your mind about memory – literally. They will enhance the way your memory works and improve your capability to learn and remember, far beyond your current levels.

Memory is not the exclusive domain of the young, and your memory does not have to decline as you get older. The techniques in this book, if used regularly, will provide a 'workout for the mind' that will keep your neurons in shape for many decades to come!

The power of recall

⦿ How well can you recall information?
⦿ Can you remember all the facts?
⦿ Can you put all the elements in the right order?

The following word recall exercise will show you some interesting things about how your brain works and how it recalls information.

The word recall exercise

Opposite is a list of words. Read each word on this list once, quickly, in order. Then turn to page 22, following, and fill in as many of the words as you can. Unless you are a grandmaster of memory, you will not be able to remember all of them, so simply try for as many as possible.

Read the complete list, one word after the other. To ensure you do this properly use a small card, covering each word as you read it.

When you have finished, turn the page to answer a few questions that will show you how your memory works.

house
floor
wall
glass
roof
tree
sky
road
and
of
the
of
and
rope
watch
Shakespeare
ring
and
of
the
table
pen
flower
pain
dog

Now fill in as many of the words, in order, as you can, without referring to the original list.

house

wall

glass

floor

dog

shakespeare

and

of

the

road

sky

Recall during learning

⊙ How many words from the beginning of the list did you remember?

_____

⊙ How many words from the end of the list did you remember?

_____

⊙ Did you recall any words that appeared more than once?

_____

⊙ Were there any words in the list that stood out in your memory as outstandingly different?

_____

⊙ How many words from the middle of the list did you remember (that you have not already noted)?

_____

In this test almost everyone recalls similar information:

⊙ One to seven words from the beginning of the list.
⊙ One or two words from the end of the list.
⊙ Most of the words that appear more than once (in this case: _the_, _and_, _of_).
⊙ The outstanding word or phrase (in this case: _Shakespeare_).
⊙ Relatively few, if any, words from the middle of the list.

Why should this similarity occur? This pattern of results shows that **memory** and **understanding** do not work in the same way: although all the words were understood, not all of them were remembered. Our ability to _recall_ information we understand is related to several factors:

⊙ We tend to remember *First things* and *Last things* more easily than things in between. Therefore we *recall more* information from the beginning and the end of a learning period. (See how the curve of the graph on page 26 begins high at the **start**, drops before the three peaks, and lifts again before the **end**.)

In the case of the word recall test, the words: house and dog appear at the beginning and the end of the sequence.

⊙ We learn more when things are A*ssociated* or *Linked* in some way: by using rhyme, repetition, or something that connects with our senses. (See points **A**, **B**, **C** on the graph opposite.)

In the case of the word recall test, repetitive words include: the, of, and; associated words are: Shakespeare and pen; or house, wall, glass and roof.

⊙ We also learn more when things are *Outstanding* or *Unique*. (See point **O** on the graph opposite: named the Von Restorff Effect, after the psychologist who discovered this fact.)

In the word recall test, the outstanding word is: Shakespeare.

Once you have read the chapter on Memory Systems, you will develop other ideas of how to link associations to remember this sequence.

The best time period in which we can recall and understand the most has been found to be between **20** and **60** minutes after the starting point. A shorter period does not give your mind long enough to assimilate what is being learned.

This will make sense to all of us. Whether studying, in a lesson or a meeting, on the telephone or in concentrated conversation, it is difficult to maintain full attention and interest for longer than 20 to 50 minutes. You will usually find that you have paused for a break, have changed the direction of the discussion, or have stopped altogether by the end of that time.

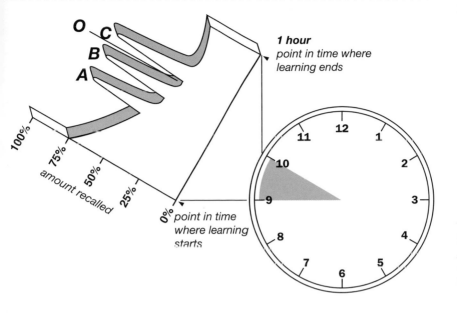

Recall *during* learning. Graph indicating that we recall more from the beginning and ends of a learning period. We also recall more when things are associated or linked (A, B and C) and more when things are outstanding or unique (O).

Taking breaks is important

Short, carefully spaced breaks are an important part of the learning and memory process. We find it easier to recall information accurately when learning if we take breaks briefly and regularly, because breaks allow your mind time to absorb what has been learned. The graph overleaf shows three different patterns of recall over a two-hour period of learning.

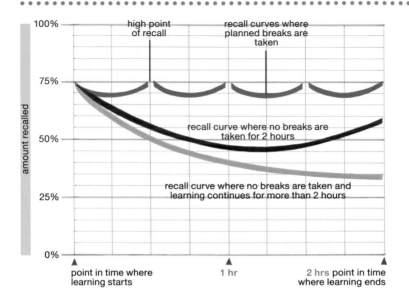

The top line includes four short breaks. The raised peaks show the moments when recall is highest. There are more high points on this line than any of the other memory curves because there are four 'beginnings and endings'. Recall remains high.

The middle line shows a recall curve when no break is taken. The beginning and end points show the highest level of recall, but overall the retention drops to well below 75 per cent.

The bottom line shows what happens if no break is taken for a period of two hours. This approach is obviously counter-productive as the recall line falls steadily downwards, to below the 50 per cent mark.

Without rests, our recall goes steadily downhill.

The more well-spaced, short breaks we have, the more beginnings and endings we have, and the better our brain will be able to remember.

⊙ Brief breaks are also essential for relaxation: they relieve the muscular and mental tension that inevitably builds up during periods of intense concentration.

The value of repetition

New information is stored first in your *short-term memory*. To transfer information to your *long-term memory* takes rehearsal and practice. On average, you will need to repeat an action at least five times before the information is transferred permanently to your long-term memory; this means revisiting what you have learned using one or more of the memory techniques on a regular basis.

My recommendations are to review and repeat what you have learned:

⊙ Shortly after you have learned it.
⊙ One day after you have learned it.
⊙ One week after you first learned it.
⊙ One month after you first learned it.
⊙ Three to six months after you first learned it.

With each period of recall, you are not only revisiting the information that you have learned; you will also be adding to your knowledge. Your creative imagination has a part to play in long-term memory, and the more you go over information you have learned, the more you will link it to other information and knowledge that you already retain:

⊙ The more we learn, the more we remember!
⊙ The more we remember, the more we learn!

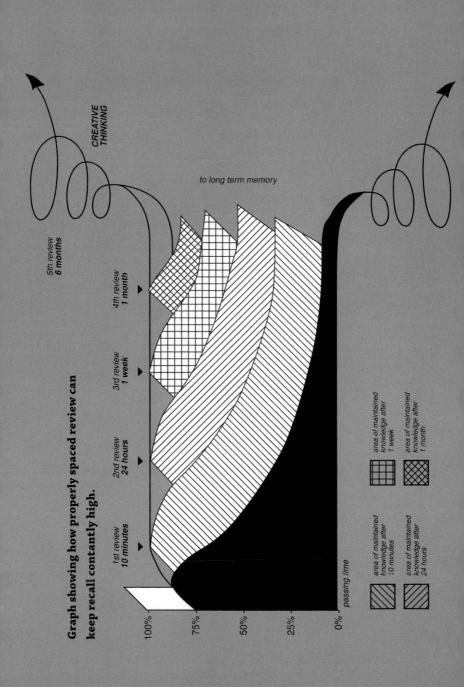

Graph showing how properly spaced review can keep recall constantly high.

CREATIVE THINKING

5th review
6 months

4th review
1 month

3rd review
1 week

2nd review
24 hours

1st review
10 minutes

to long term memory

100%

75%

50%

25%

0%

passing time

area of maintained knowledge after 10 minutes

area of maintained knowledge after 24 hours

area of maintained knowledge after 1 week

area of maintained knowledge after 1 month

3 THE CORE MEMORY PRINCIPLES

In Greek and Roman times, leading senators used displays of their memory to impress constituents and each other with their feats of learning and genius. Long before anything was known about the brain and how it functions, the ancient Greeks realized that memory works by linking information. They were the first to discover the two essential foundation stones, fundamental to the process of memory:

Imagination   Association

Two Fundamental Memory Principles
Imagination
The more you stimulate and use your *Imagination*, the more you will enhance your ability to learn. This is because your imagination has no limits; it is boundless and it stimulates your senses, and therefore your brain. Having an unlimited imagination makes you more open to new experiences and less inclined to hold yourself back from learning new things.

Association
The most effective way to remember something is to think about it as an image, in *Association* with something else that is already fixed and known to you. If you ground your images in reality by associating them with something that is familiar, it will anchor them in a *location,* and you will be able to remember the information more easily.

Association works by linking or pegging information to other information.

For example: if you think about a banana you will associate it with the colour yellow, its country of origin, its shape, its taste, where you might buy it, where you store it.

You will have an *image* of the banana, and a *location* for it. Association works in partnership with your Imagination.

Imagination and Association are at the heart of all the techniques in this book – they are the foundation stones upon which memory techniques are based. The more effectively you can use them, through key memory devices such as words, numbers and images, the more supercharged and effective your mind and memory will be.

As explained on page 12, for your brain to work effectively you need to use both sides of your brain: the left side and the right side. It can be no coincidence that the two foundation stones of memory coincide with two main activities of the brain:

Imagination }
             Together they = **MEMORY**
Association }

Your memory gives you your sense of who you are, and so it is appropriate that the mnemonic to remember this is:

I AM

Imagination and Association are supported by the Core Memory Principles. These principles help to anchor events in your memory and make it easier to recall them on demand.

In addition to associating with something familiar, to remember something effectively your memory also needs to have: a wonderful, multicoloured, multisensory *image* in mind that stimulates your imagination, your senses and brings your memory alive.

The Memory Systems described in Chapter 5 create Key Words that are transformed into Key Images that use *image* and *location* to make them effective. They use all 12 of the Core Memory Principles. The next section describes the ten further Essential Memory Principles that work together with the foundation principles of Imagination and Association to encourage your memory to work to optimum effectiveness.

Ten Essential Memory Principles

To superpower your memory and help it to recall information efficiently, you will need to use every aspect of your mind. The Essential Memory Principles are designed to reinforce the strength of the impact of Imagination and Association on memory, and to trigger the involvement of as much of your extraordinary brainpower as possible.

The ten memory principles that are used together with Imagination and Association are:

1 Your senses   **2 Exaggeration**
3 Rhythm and movement   **4 Colour**
5 Numbers   **6 Symbols**
7 Order and patterns   **8 Attraction**
9 Laughter   **10 Positive thinking**

The difference in impact is rather like using a 15-million-candlepower spotlight instead of your standard 4.5-volt battery torch to illuminate your way home. You would experience the world more brightly and more brilliantly than ever before.

The Memory Principles are also designed to encourage the use of other elements that are necessary for recall: such as sensual triggers and extraordinary images.

Using your creative Imagination

Your imagination is fed by information and influences via the right side of your brain. Extraordinary memories and those that stand out in some way are the ones that can be recalled more easily and effectively (see page 24).

The following Principles have especial impact on the power and functioning of your memory:

1   Senses

The more you can visualize, hear, taste, smell, feel or sense the thing that you are trying to recall, the better you will reinforce your ability to remember and be able to call to mind the information when you need it.

Everything you experience, everything you learn and everything you enjoy, is delivered to your brain via your senses:

Vision   Hearing   Smell
Taste   Touch
Spatial awareness – of your body and its movement

The more sensitive you become to the information that your senses receive, the better you will be able to remember.

The sense of smell is a common trigger for childhood memories. How many of us have been taken back to childhood unexpectedly by the smell of floor polish at a school, or the scent of a particular shrub or a perfume? This sense will be accompanied by a sudden and perfectly clear memory of people or events from a previous time in your life that has been stored in your brain for years.

⊙ Your *sense of smell* and *sense of place* are triggers that release memory.

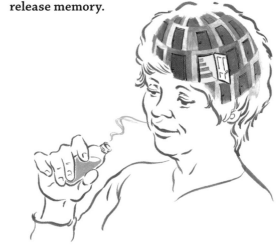

2 Exaggeration

Think large and be absurd in your imaginings. The more exaggerated your images are, in size, shape and sound, the better you will be able to remember them. Think of children's favourite characters: the cartoon ogre, Shrek, and the *Harry Potter* giant, Hagrid, are larger than life and stay alive in the mind's eye more readily than other characters in the films (see page 24).

3 Rhythm and movement

Movement adds to the potential for something to be memorable to your brain.

- Make your images move.
- Make them three-dimensional.
- Give them rhythm.

Movement helps your brain to 'link in' to the story and will help the sequence of data to become more extraordinary, and therefore memorable.

4 Colour

Colour brings memories alive and makes events more memorable. Whenever possible, use colour in your imaginings and in your drawings and notes so that your visual sense is heightened and your brain is stimulated to enjoy the experience of seeing.

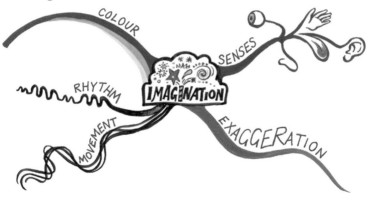

Using the power of Association

Associations anchor memories and concepts, making it easier to access them again. They are a vital part of enabling imaginative thought to transform into creative memories. Associations are helped by the use of:

5 Numbers

Numbers have a powerful impact on your memory because they bring order to your thoughts. Numbers help to make memories more specific.

6 Symbols

Symbols are a compact and coded way of using Imagination and Exaggeration to anchor memory. Creating a symbol to prompt a memory is rather like creating a logo. It tells a story and connects to, and is representative of, something larger than the image itself.

7 Order and patterns

Ordering your thoughts or putting them in sequence can be very useful when used in conjunction with other memory principles. You might think about grouping thoughts by colour, weight or size, or order items by height, age or location.

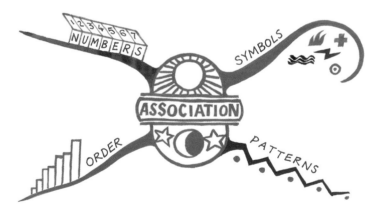

Using both sides of your brain

When the Memory Principles are used to their full extent, both sides of your brain work more effectively and have a powerful and positive effect on each other. (See also pages 12–13.)

There are three further principles that are as important as those listed opposite, and which have a powerful impact on both sides of your brain:

8   Attraction

We know what we like to look at and how we feel when we are attracted to someone or something. Your mind will remember an attractive image more readily than an unattractive one. Use your imagination to include attractive, positive images and associations as part of your memory.

9   Laughter

The more we laugh, the more we enjoy thinking about what we want to remember, and the easier it is to summon up information. Use humour, absurdity and a sense of fun to enhance your ability to remember and recall.

10 Positive thinking

In most instances, it is easier and more pleasant to recall positive images and experiences than negative ones. This is because your brain wants to return to things that make you feel good about life and positive about your experiences. Negative associations

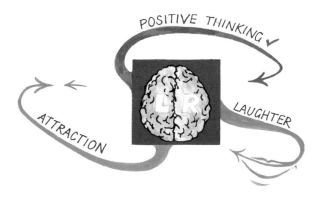

and experiences are more likely to be blocked or modified by your brain. Think positive, and your imagination and associations will have more positive power.

The next chapter explains the role of Key Words and Numbers and how they can be transformed into Key Images that will be triggers for recalling Key Memories.

The memory principles just discussed make use of the fundamental principles of Imagination and Association to create connections between pairs of words/images, and connect them in ways that are clear and uncomplicated.

There are some basic rules about creating effective connections; following them makes the difference between creating an interesting moment that you will later forget, or establishing a core, lasting memory:

When creating connections between Key Images, remember that you can:

- *Crash* things together.
- *Stick* things together.
- Place things *on top* of each other.
- Place things *underneath* each other.
- Place things *inside* each other.
- *Substitute* things for each other.
- Place things in *new situations*.
- *Wrap* things together.
- Have things *talk*.
- Have things *dance*.
- Have things *sharing* their *colour*, *aroma* or *action*.

4 UNLOCK YOUR MEMORY WITH KEY WORDS AND IMAGES

Your memory finds images easier to recall than words or numbers. From birth until the time you learned to speak and read, your early associations were made by observation: you understood the image 'apple' before you understood the word 'apple'; a warm smile or a tone of voice had a more immediate impact than the choice of words. As an adult, when you learn a new language, you are likely to supplement communication with symbols and pictures because you don't have the vocabulary of speech.

For that reason, in every Memory System, a *Key Image* is chosen that becomes synonymous with a *Key Word* or *Number*. The Key Words or Numbers will trigger the recall of that Key Image in your memory, and the Key Image will in turn trigger recall of the word or number.

These triggers are the pegs on which you will learn to hang all the other items you want to remember.

Key

The Word 'Key' in front of the words Number, Word or Image means much more than 'this is important'. It means this is a 'Memory Key'. The Key Word, Key Number or Key Image is being developed as a critically important trigger to stimulate your mind, and to unlock and retrieve your memories.

Key Word

A Key Word is a special word that has been chosen or created to become a unique reference point for something important that you wish to remember. Words stimulate the left side of the brain and are a vital component of mastering memory; they are not as powerful on their own as when you take the time to draw them and transform them into Key Images. Only when Key Words become Key Images do they stimulate both sides of your brain.

Key Image

Key Images are the cornerstones of memory and are called *Key Memory Word Images* in my Mind Set books (see Further Reading) because they are carefully constructed word-image composites of vital importance in releasing deeply-stored memory. A Key Image is much, much more than a picture. It is an image that is linked to and associated with a Key Word and/or a Key Number. It has been created, using the Memory Principles, to stimulate your imagination and recreate familiar associations. An effective Key Image will stimulate both sides of your brain and draw upon all your senses. Key Images are at the very heart of Buzan Memory Techniques.

Key Number

Key Numbers feature mainly in the Major Number System and the Card Memory System. They are transformed into Key Words before being transformed into a Key Image.

There are five memory systems explained in this book, each of which relies on these fundamental principles. I will introduce you to all of these in Chapter 5.

At their root are two important *memory trigger* systems:

Link Systems   **Peg Systems**

Link Systems

A Link System is the most basic of all memory systems. It transforms Key Words into Key Images and links them together by using a 'story-telling' approach. It is ideal for memorizing short lists of items, such as shopping lists. The system makes important use of *Imagination* and *Association*, and uses the

Memory Principles (see page 30). The method encourages the use of all your senses and enhances the connections between the imaginative and logical functions of your brain.

The Link Story System

There are three principle guidelines for constructing a Link Story. They are:

⦿ Simplicity: keep the story unencumbered by detail.

⦿ Clarity: keep the descriptions clear and straightforward.

⦿ One to one: link each item to only one other (refer to the guidelines on page 38 for ways to do this).

The Link Story System in action

Since the Link System is ideal for memorizing items that you may have on a typical shopping list, your Key Word list may include things such as:

○ **Frozen chicken**

○ **Brown eggs**

○ **Toothpaste**

○ **Cat food**

○ **Cling film**

○ **Cauliflower**

○ **Pudding rice**

○ **Soap powder**

○ **Clothes pegs**

○ **A birthday card**

Read through the list now, once only, trying to memorize both the items and the order in which they are listed. Then turn to page 44 and see how many items you can reproduce and in the correct order.

You will probably find that the Key Words on their own are difficult to recall. Even though they represent familiar and everyday items, the chances are you will not remember all the words initially, and will find recalling them in correct sequence a challenge.

You will find that you achieve a much better result if you

transform the Key Words into Key Images because your brain can remember pictures more easily than words on their own.

Instead of writing everything down on a list (that you then leave at home by mistake!), I would like you to create a story that draws upon your imagination and creates associations between each of the items. The more wild and absurd you can make the links, the more likely you are to remember all the items on the list.

For example:

Imagine that you are walking along the road with an enormous **chicken** that is nearly as tall as you. *Listen* to her loud clucks and be aware of the *feel* of her heavy feathers, which are **frozen** and covered in icicles. The icicles clank together and are slowly melting as she walks.

The chicken is walking very slowly because she is pulling behind her a straw nest filled with beautiful fresh, speckled, **brown eggs**.

Sitting on the eggs, and trying not to crush them, is the chicken farmer. He has a broad *smile* and gleaming teeth which he is brushing with bright green **toothpaste**.

The farmer is balancing three tins of **cat food** on his head which *wobble* precariously each time the chicken clucks. He wears a raincoat made of **cling film** that is billowing in the wind. The movement makes you look up to the sky.

To your amazement, the cloud above you has leafy green edges and you *see* that it is an enormous, crisp, white, crunchy **cauliflower**: the largest you have ever seen.

From the sky, **pudding rice** begins to fall, turning into sugary puddles of dessert as it reaches the pavement. You can *smell* its sweet scent as you lift your feet. It is a very sticky situation!

At that moment a young man drives up in a cardboard car made from a box of **soap powder**. The doors are held together with multi-coloured **clothes pegs**.

He leaps out, skids in the rice pudding, and hands the farmer a **birthday card**!

It is a silly story and the stuff of children's tales or wild dreams, but by this method each familiar item is linked in an exaggerated way to the next. The sequence involves and stimulates all your senses, with memory triggers embedded within the sequence. The triggers are:

- movement
- sequence
- colour
- attraction
- humour
- exaggeration, and
- order.

– all designed to encourage imagination and association, and engage your memory.

If you replay the sequence in your mind using Key Images enhanced by the elements listed above, you are likely to be able to recall all the items on the list – in the correct order. Fill them in the space following:

_____

_____

_____

_____

_____

_____

_____

_____

Peg Systems

A Peg System is similar to a Link System, but uses special, Key Images on which you can attach whatever you want to memorize. The Key Images are permanent memory pegs that once chosen, shouldn't change. The images work as memory anchors that 'peg down' the memory, making it simple to recall.

> **A Peg System can be thought of as being rather like a wardrobe containing a fixed number of hangers on which to put your clothes. The hangers themselves never change, but the clothes that are hung on them change constantly.**

A Peg System makes special use of numbers and order, thereby appealing very strongly to the left side of your brain (while also working in elegant partnership with the right side of your brain).

These memory trigger techniques are at the heart of all the Memory Systems that follow in the next chapter.

5 FIVE KEY MEMORY SYSTEMS

This chapter will introduce you to five super-powered memory systems that have been used successfully by generations of memory masters. They are:

The Number–Shape System
The Number–Rhyme System
The Alphabet System
The Memory Room
The Name–Face System

The combined force of these systems will enable you to remember anything you wish to, from the birthdays of all your friends, to shopping lists, historical dates and other essentials.

The Number–Shape System

⊙ The Number–Shape System is a Peg System, as described in Chapter 4.

⊙ It is ideal for short-term memory use, for recalling those items that you need to remember only for a few hours.

⊙ Each of the numbers is anchored to a constant set of images that you choose yourself.

The Number–Shape System is simple. All you have to do is think of an image for each of the numbers from one to ten. Young children around the world spend time making pictures out of numbers as they doodle in maths lessons. It is an interesting instinct. The brain *naturally* encourages us to find ways of remembering information.

I will explain how to construct the system and will give you examples. As we are all different, the images that will work best for you are ones that you choose and create for yourself. Once you understand the system, modify the words and images to fit your own imagination.

Each Key Image acts as a visual reminder of the number with which it is associated. Images should be strong and simple: easy to draw, easy to visualize and remember. The following list of associations shows classic examples.

1 **paintbrush**
2 **swan**
3 **heart**
4 **yacht**
5 **hook**
6 **elephant's trunk**
7 **cliff**
8 **snowman**
9 **balloon and stick**
10 **bat and ball**

After practising, you will automatically see in your mind's eye the image of a yacht, for example, when you think of the number four; or a swan when you think of the number two.

Each of us is different and so the numbers will conjure up different images for different people. Give yourself about ten minutes to think of any other alternatives that you may prefer to those listed above and choose the one image for each number that works best for you. These will become *your* Key Number–Shape Memory *images*.

Use the space provided opposite to write each number and draw the images that you have chosen to represent each digit.

- *Don't* worry about how 'good' or 'bad' the images are.
- *Do* use colour to bring the images alive and to reinforce them in your memory.
- *Do* use also exaggeration, and movement.

When you have completed the task, close your eyes and run through the numbers from one to ten to ensure that you have remembered each of the image associations.

Then count backwards from ten to one, doing the same thing.

Practise recalling numbers at random until the Number–Shape image association becomes second nature.

The idea is that the *image*, rather than the number, will gradually become synonymous with the numerical order.

Once you are comfortable that you can instantly recall the Number–Shape images, you can begin to use them in daily life. Simply peg the Number–Shape images to other words and then link them together by creating imaginative associations.

The Number–Shape System in action

Take a look at the following list of items:

1   symphony
2   prayer
3   watermelon
4   volcano

5   motorcycle
6   sunshine
7   apple pie
8   blossoms
9   spaceship
10 field of wheat

⊙ In your mind's eye, think of the Number–Shape images on page 50 that you have chosen to represent the numbers one to ten.
⊙ Now peg those Key Images to each of the words in the list above.
⊙ Then create an imaginative image to link each of the pegged pairings.
⊙ Create associations that are outrageous, crazy and colourful, so that you are better able to remember them.

For example, when paired with the words on the list, my Number–Shape memory keys are:

1 **paintbrush**	+ symphony
2 **swan**	+ prayer
3 **heart**	+ watermelon
4 **yacht**	+ volcano
5 **hook**	+ motorcycle
6 **elephant's trunk**	+ sunshine
7 **cliff**	+ apple pie
8 **snowman**	+ blossoms
9 **balloon and stick**	+ spaceship
10 **bat and ball**	+ field of wheat

The links could become:
⊙ For *symphony* you might imagine a conductor, conducting frantically, with a gigantic **paintbrush**.

◉ *Prayer* is an abstract word, which can be represented by adding form to the image. Try imagining your **swan** with its wings upheld like hands in prayer.

◉ With a little imagination your *watermelon* can be transformed into a **heart**-shaped fruit, beating.

◉ Imagine a gigantic *volcano* within the ocean that erupts red and furious beneath your **yacht**.

◉ Imagine a heavy **hook** coming down from the sky and lifting you and your speeding *motorcycle* off the road.

◉ Imagine rays of *sunshine* pouring out of an **elephant's trunk**.

◉ Your **cliff** could be made entirely of *apple pie*.

◉ Imagine a **snowman** in springtime covered from head to foot in sweet *blossoms.*

◉ Imagine a minature **spaceship** that has flown into your *balloon and stick* and caused it to burst.

◉ Imagine the shock as your **bat** cracks against the **ball**, and the ball is sent flying across a golden and windswept *field of wheat.*

You get the idea.

It is when you start to create your own sequences that you will feel this technique working. Don't just read the examples given here; create your own. The more absurd, over-the-top and sensual you are able to make your associations, the better you will tap into your own imagination. The more you practise, the easier the technique will be, and eventually, it will become second nature.

Memory bites

◉ Refer to the Core Memory Principles (Chapter 3) for a reminder of all the different elements to include in your Pegged pairs.

◉ The more surreal and exaggerated you can make the image, the more memorable it will be.

⊙ As with the Link System, you will get more value from the Peg System if you practise. (The tests in Chapter 6 are designed to help you hone your technique.)

⊙ Remember to make the connections between the images strong.

⊙ Abstract words can be remembered by giving them concrete form. For example, 'thinking' can be represented by an image, such as a lightbulb or Rodin's *The Thinker*.

The Number–Rhyme System

The Number–Rhyme System is easy to learn and is based on a similar principle to the Number–Shape System. It is ideal for use when you need to remember short lists of items for a brief period of time.

⊙ The Number–Rhyme System differs from the Number–Shape System only in that it uses *rhyming sounds* rather than associated shapes as memory triggers for the numbers one to ten.

⊙ The words you choose should conjure up *strong but simple images*, be easy to draw and easy to visualize and remember.

The following list of rhyming words will start you off. (I will be using these words to illustrate the example, following.)

1   **bun**
2   **shoe**
3   **tree**
4   **door**
5   **hive**
6   **sticks**
7   **heaven**
8   **skate**
9   **vine**
10 **hen**

Please use your imagination, if you wish different images, to come up with alternative, memorable rhymes that work for you.

As with the Link Story System (pages 42–4) and the Number–Shape System (pages 48–53), it is important to use as many of the Memory Principles as possible to help make each image imaginative, colourful and appealing to your senses. The more extraordinary and memorable you can make the images, the better your mind will remember them.

Choose words that are easy for you to remember and associate with each number, and draw your image in the boxes on the next page – using as much colour and imagination as possible.

⊙ To help create the clearest mental picture possible for each image, close your eyes and imagine projecting the image onto the inside of your eyelid – or to a screen inside your head.

⊙ Hear, feel, smell or experience the image that works best for you.

When you have completed the task, close your eyes and run through the numbers from one to ten to ensure that you have remembered each of the rhyming image associations. Then count backwards from ten to one, doing the same thing.

The faster you are able to do this, the better your memory will become. The more you practise these techniques, the more your associative and creative thinking abilities will improve.

⊙ Practise recalling numbers at random until the Number–Rhymes and image association becomes second-nature.

The Number–Rhyme System in action

Once you have memorized your Number–Rhyme Key Words and Images you will be ready to put the Number–Rhyme System into action. Start by using the list of items below:

1 table
2 feather
3 cat
4 leaf
5 student
6 orange
7 car
8 pencil
9 shirt
10 poker

Refer back to page 55 and you will see that the Number–Rhyme pairings would become:

1	**bun**	+ table
2	**shoe**	+ feather
3	**tree**	+ cat
4	**door**	+ leaf
5	**hive**	+ student
6	**sticks**	+ orange
7	**heaven**	+ car
8	**skate**	+ pencil
9	**vine**	+ shirt
10	**hen**	+ poker

The Key Words are in bold. These are your memory triggers and remain consistent, no matter what else you are trying to remember.

Use Imagination and Association to create links between the pairs of words, perhaps as follows:

⊙ **1** Imagine a giant **bun** on top of a fragile *table* which is in the process of crumbling from the weight. Smell the fresh cooked aroma, taste your favourite bun.

⊙ **2** Imagine your favourite **shoe** with an enormous feather growing out of the inside, preventing you from putting your shoe on, tickling your feet.

⊙ **3** Imagine a large **tree** with either your own *cat* or a cat you know, stuck in the very top branches, frantically scrambling about and mewing loudly.

⊙ **4** Imagine your bedroom **door** is a giant *leaf*, crunching and rustling as you open it.

⊙ **5** Imagine a *student* at his desk, dressed in black and yellow stripes, buzzing busily in a **hive** of activity, or with honey dripping on his pages.

⊙ **6** Imagine large **sticks** puncturing the juicy surface of an orange that is as big as a beach ball. Feel and smell the juice of the orange squirting out.

⊙ **7** Imagine all the angels in **heaven** sitting on cars rather than clouds; experience yourself driving the car you consider to be heavenly.

⊙ **8** Imagine yourself **skating** over the pavement, hearing the sound of the wheels on the ground, as you see the multi-coloured *pencils* attached to your skates creating fantastic coloured shapes wherever you go.

⊙ **9** Imagine a **vine** as large as Jack and the Beanstalk's bean stalk , and instead of leaves on the vine, picture brightly coloured *shirts* hanging all over it, blowing in the wind.

⊙ **10** Now it's your turn .... Imagine a **hen**, with a *poker* ...

Memory bites

To improve your application of the technique, go back over the examples and make sure that all the Memory Principles are being used. Check that all the word and image associations are strong, positive, simple and clear, and make sure they are working for you. Ask:

- ⦿ Are there any associations that may become attractive?
- ⦿ Is there enough distance between the associations?
- ⦿ Do they need more exaggeration and imagination?
- ⦿ Do they need more colour?
- ⦿ Do they need more movement?
- ⦿ Are the links between the images strong enough?
- ⦿ Is there enough sensuality?
- ⦿ Is there enough humour?

You can be sure that each time you practise, your technique will improve fast, and your memory will perform well above average.

Having learned both the Number–Shape System and the Number–Rhyme System, you have not only two separate 1–10 systems, but also two systems that can be combined to memorize a sequence of up to twenty items.

Simply use one system (e.g. The Number–Rhyme System) to represent numbers 1–10 and the other (e.g. the Number-Shape System) to represent the numbers 11–20.

The Alphabet System

The Alphabet System is a Peg System that is similar to the Number–Shape and Number–Rhyme Systems in the way that it works; the difference is that it uses the *sounds* of the names of the letters of the alphabet as memory pegs, instead of numbers.

To begin, you first select Key Words that start with the *sound* of the letter you want to remember.
- Make sure the word is easy to remember.
- Make sure the word is easy to imagine.
- Make sure the word is simple to draw.

Wherever possible, use a word that:
- *'Spells'* the sound of the letter.

For example: Bee (for the letter 'B').
  Or:
- *Sounds like* the letter:

For example: Sea (for the letter 'C').

Avoid using words that start with the letter, but don't sound like the letter.

For example: Ant (begins with *short* a, not *long* a), Car (begins with a *hard* c, not a *soft* c).

Transform your Key Word into a Key Image by drawing it. This becomes your memory peg on which to hang the things you want to remember.

In order for the system to work at its best for you, you should choose your own words. The following are some easy suggestions to start you off:

Letter/ Sound		Word that starts with the sound	Picture suggestion
A	*ay*	*Ace*	The ace of spades
B	*bee*	*Bee*	A buzzing bee
C	*see*	*Sea*	The seashore
D	*dee*	*Deed*	A legal document with seal
E	*ee*	*Easel*	An artist at work
F	*eff*	*Effervescence*	A glass of bubbly water
G	*gee*	*Jeep*	The army vehicle
H	*ay-ch*	*H-bomb*	An explosion
I	*i-ye*	*Eye*	An open eye
J	*jay*	*Jay*	The songbird
K	*kay*	*Cake*	(sounds like 'K') A large cake
L	*el*	*Elbow*	A bent arm
M	*em*	*MC*	Initials of Master of Ceremonies
N	*en*	*Enamel*	A brooch
O	*oh*	*Oboe*	The musical instrument
P	*pee*	*Pea*	A pea loose from its pod
Q	*kew*	*Queue*	People in a row
R	*ah-r*	*Arch*	A roman archway
S	*ess*	*Eskimo*	Head with fluffy hood
T	*tee*	*Tea*	A teapot
U	*yoo*	*Yew*	The tree
V	*vee*	*Vehicle*	A red bus
W	*double-yoo*	WC	Ladies and men's signs
X	*ex*	*X-ray*	A rib-cage in a frame
Y	*wiy*	*Wife*	A woman
Z	*zed*	*Zebra*	A zebra in a Prairie

Once you are happy with your selection of words and images, and you feel that they are pictures that you would enjoy recalling as memory triggers, practise using them.

⊙ Draw the images yourself so you can use them as a visual reference and help bed them firmly into your memory.

⊙ It is useful to draw each image on separate sheets of paper, or card, so that you can review them in any order. (You could put a letter on one side of the page and the corresponding image on the other, so that it is easier to test yourself.)

⊙ Practise visualizing the images in sequential order, reverse order, and random order, so you can recall them on demand.

The Alphabet System in action

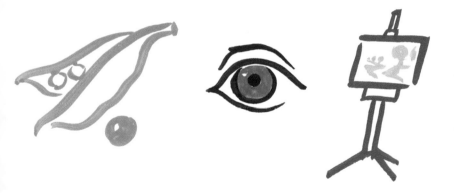

See page 81 for a simple Memory Test that will help you to assess your progress with this system.

The Memory Room

The Romans were highly ordered and organized people with a strong aesthetic sense and a liking for opulent surroundings. They were great inventors of memory techniques and competitions, and one of their most popular and highly successful techniques is the Memory Room.

The Memory Room appeals to both sides of your brain because it combines order and precision with imagination and beauty. It is a combined link and peg system that allows you to place as many objects as you like inside the house of your dreams. Each object and item of furniture is placed in the house in a very precise way. Each item is placed carefully and permanently in its ideal position, and each one acts as a link to those items you wish to remember.

As you approach the house and your memory room, imagine it very precisely. See yourself walking through the front gate, along the path, up a number of front steps, and in through the door. As you build your room, make sure that you travel in your imagination in order from item to item.

For example:

An elegant Roman room has two enormous marble pillars either side of the doorway; there is a carved lion's head on the door and a large Greek statue to the left of the door as you walk in. Next to the statue there is a *sofa* covered in fur; next to the sofa is a large flowering plant and, in front of the sofa is a solid marble table on which are placed two wine goblets, a carafe of wine and a bowl of fruit.

Each of these items becomes a Key Image that will trigger a memory. (See the image on page 82 for a representation of this example.)

In the same way that the Key Images in the Number–Shape system become the baseline links to the items you want to remember, so too, when using the Memory Room method, the items in the room become the permanent triggers that are connected and associated with the items you want to remember.

Need to remember to order flowers for your mother's birthday? Imagine a Roman centurion festooning the pillars with spring flowers, smelling the blooms and filling the room with scent.

Need to remember to take your ice skates with you for the weekend? Imagine a mischievous boy skating on the marble table top, and sending the goblets flying.

The advantages of the Memory Room are:
◉ It lends itself naturally to using all the Memory Principles (pages 30–8).
◉ It is entirely imaginary, so you can leave in the room every wonderful object that you could possibly desire and include music, scents, flavours and textures that appeal to all your senses.
◉ You will begin to believe on a deep level that you own some of these objects, which will programme your mind and your memory to help you acquire them, if you so wish.
◉ The Memory Room holds no boundaries, so your imagination can run riot, stimulating the right side of your brain.
◉ The Memory Room requires order and precision, so it also appeals strongly to the left side of your brain.

Memory bites

◉ Jot down *your ideas* about the shape and design of your room, the types of objects you want in it and where you would like to put them.

◉ Then *draw a plan* or a picture of your room and add the names of the objects and where you would like to put them.

◉ Start with putting ten items in the room, in very *specific locations*.

◉ Take a few *'mental walks'* around your room, using the link system to memorize precisely the order, position and number of items in the room.

◉ Make sure you practise using *all of your senses* to experience the colours, textures, smells and sounds within the room. This is your mental warm-up and fixes the information deeper into your memory.

◉ When you are confident that the location and type of each object is second nature, you can begin to use each of them as the 'pegs' on which to hang the list of items you want to remember.

◉ When you are used to working with these, move up to 15, 20, 30 items in your memory room, and so on.

◉ You can *add as many rooms as you wish* and transform your room into a house, castle, palace, village – or galaxy – if you want to.

There are *no limits* to your imagination or your memory!

The Memory Room in action

Many people find that this is their favourite memory system. If you like drawing, it's an excellent idea to illustrate your memory room. Try drawing the layout of the room and the objects within it to help cement the contents and location of each item in your memory.

Turn to page 82 for a Self-Test related to the Memory Room.

The Name–Face system

If your memory has trouble linking names and faces, it is for a good reason: there may be no obvious logical connection between what someone looks like or what they do, and what they are called. Your mind therefore has more difficulty making natural associations that will feed the logical side of your brain. You need to exercise your imagination to encourage both sides of your brain to work together more effectively.

In times past it was easier to remember people because their names and occupations offered clear clues. Mr Baker was a baker, Mrs Meatyard was the farmer's wife, Mr Lowton probably lived at the bottom end of town and Mr Robertson was the son of Mr Roberts. Added to which, generations of families lived in the same district, which probably meant that there were recognizable physiological traits present in members of the same family (such as their nose, eyes, and ears, etc).

Multiple memories

A team of psychologists showed a group of people a selection of 1000 photographs, displaying them at one image per second. The psychologists then chose 100 of the photographs that had been shown, and combined them with 100 photographs that had not been shown to the group. They asked each person to recall two things: whether they had seen the photograph earlier, and in what order the photographs had been shown. Amazingly, *everyone* in the group was able to identify *almost* every photograph correctly – even those people who said they had bad memories!

The group were less successful in ranking the

> photographs in the right order. It seems the memory
> really does 'never forget a face' – although it can find
> attaching the right name to the face more of a challenge.
> ⊙ *Images* are more effective *memory triggers* than
> words or numbers on their own.

In modern times you need to create your own associations to
help you to remember the people you meet. There are two basic
techniques to achieve this, each of which supports the other:

The social method
For this to be successful you need:
⊙ A genuine interest in the people you meet
⊙ Respect for who they are, and
⊙ courtesy in conversation.
See the techniques below for how to put this into practice.

The mnemonic method
This technique uses:

Imagination   **Association**

(These concepts are explained in Chapter 3, and were applied
in the previous four systems in this chapter via the Key Words
and Images.)

The difference between the Name–Face System and the
previous four systems is that you already have your Key Image
staring you in the face! So with this technique you need to
devise imaginative visual triggers that your brain can interpret
into Key Words instead: i.e. the person's name, via association.

Using these methods you need never again feel the embarrassment of forgetting someone's name moments after having been introduced or, surely worse, forgetting the name of someone you have known for years while introducing them to others at a social function!

The social method

In order to be successful, the social method requires you to be genuinely interested in those you meet and to be an attentive listener.

Choose your mind set

If meeting new people makes you nervous, or you regularly tell yourself that you can never remember people's names, then you need to prepare yourself mentally in advance. Tell yourself that you have a *good* memory and that you have the techniques to recall people's names with 100 per cent accuracy. The more you believe it, the more relaxed you will be. The more relaxed you are, the more the technique will succeed. If in doubt, give yourself a few minutes to relax and prepare yourself before you put yourself in the situation.

Look and see

Memory relies upon images, so you need to learn really to *see* the person to whom you are speaking. No matter how shy you are or how casual the encounter, look the person in the eye when you meet them, and be aware of any special facial characteristics they may have – from the top of their head, to the tip of their chin. (See pages 74–6 for more details of this technique.)

The more you sharpen your powers of observation, and the more connected you are to the moment of meeting, the stronger your memory of that moment. A first meeting is a first impression – and an important moment for reinforcing memory.

With practice you will come to identify the differences between people and what makes one different from another. This practice will help you to hone the technique.

Listen carefully

Consciously listening to the sound of the name of the person you are being introduced to is critical in the process of learning a new name. This may seem an obvious thing to say, but how many times, when being introduced, have you been preoccupied with how you look, with who else you know there, or with the fact that you might forget the name – rather than truly listening to what is being said?

Repeat the name out loud

Repetition is an important element in learning something new – and so it can be valuable to ask for the person's name to be repeated, in order to reinforce the memory – even if you think you have heard the name quite clearly.

The old-fashioned way of introducing people to one another achieves this quite naturally:

'Jennifer Smith, please meet Gareth Jones. Gareth Jones, I would like you to meet Jennifer Smith.'

Pronounce the name

As soon as you have been given the name, it is important to confirm the pronunciation – perhaps by asking the origin of the name. If the surname is fairly common, concentrate on finding associations for the first name so that it is bedded in your memory. Introduce the whole name into conversation so that you say and hear the words out loud.

Spell the name

It can help to know how the name is spelt – so ask them, in a light-hearted way, as this too gives an opportunity for repetition of the words.

Ask about personal history

Fifty per cent of people know something about the derivation of their name, or of their family history. It is easy to start a conversation about genealogy, and discussing the history of a name will further bed down the name of your new acquaintance.

Exchange information

Depending on the circumstance, the easiest way of checking the detail of someone's name is to exchange business cards. The Japanese tradition is to exchange business cards and lay them neatly in view throughout the meeting. This is a mark of respect – and has the added benefit of keeping their acquaintance's name in clear view at all times.

Repeat in conversation

Showing interest and politeness during a conversation offers a useful excuse to repeat names frequently ('Jane told me that …'; 'Paul, I'd like to congratulate you on …'). It is a more intimate way to converse and also reinforces the names even further in your memory.

Check your memory

Keep your mind engaged on the people in the room by checking with yourself at intervals that you still remember people's names and what they have told you about themselves. By this process you will re-remember what you have learned and will reinforce the names in your memory.

Repeat at parting

Because the brain remembers beginnings and endings more easily than 'middles' (see page 24), it is important to repeat the name of each person you meet as you say goodbye to them. It will not only make them feel special; it will also consolidate your learning process.

Review

It is important to go over the information that you have learned after you have parted from your new contacts or acquaintances:

Take a mental picture: Flash through your mind all the names and faces of those you have just met.

Take a real picture: In this digital age you may have taken recent photographs of everyone. Take the opportunity to look at the pictures to help reinforce your memory.

Draw and describe the picture: Drawing and writing reinforce learning. If you are really serious about improving your memory, I recommend that you keep notes, or a diary, including quick sketches of those people you have met, to gather *Key Image* and *Key Word* information – ideally using plenty of colour, movement and other triggers.

Reverse the principle

Help other people to remember you, too, by reversing the process above. Repeat your name, tell people the origins of your name, give them your card if appropriate and help them to introduce you to others by reminding them of who you are.

Pace yourself

Never rush new introductions; your nervousness will increase the chance of your forgetting new faces. Find something to say to each person you meet so that there is time for your brain to absorb the new information and so that the pace of conversation is relaxed and sociable.

Enjoy yourself
Meeting new people is interesting and opens you up to new knowledge and experiences. The more you enjoy yourself, the more relaxed your brain will become, and the more effectively it will create the imaginative associations necessary for good memory.

The plus-one principle
Most people find it hard to remember the names of more than 2–5 people out of every 30 that they meet. If this sounds like you, set yourself a personal challenge: to remember just one more person than you would normally. By practising the techniques above, you will rapidly improve your chances of success.

The mnemonic method
The mnemonic principles for remembering names and faces are the use of *Imagination* and *Association*:

Imagination
- Create a clear mental image of the person's name.
- Make sure you can 'hear' the sound of the person's name.
- Mentally reconstruct the person's face in your mind, using your imagination as a cartoonist would.
- Exaggerate in your mind's eye any distinguishing features.

Association
Study the face of the person you want to remember and find something about them that reminds you of their name.

It can be difficult to remember the names of your friends' children on occasion. You remember baby Clara because she has the same name as your aunt, but how can you remember which is Tom and which is Oliver? Teenager Tom might have a feisty attitude that reminds you of a *tom*cat raring for a fight; little Oliver might remind you of the lead character in the film *Oliver Twist*.

Your new neighbours are very nice but you can't remember whether their surname is 'Brown' or 'Green'. Look at the colour of their front door, or hair colour, or eyes. See whether there is a visual reminder that will help you to get it right.

Of course, hair styles, hair colour, clothing and door paint can change, so whenever possible, try to select reference points or features that are unlikely to change.

How to read faces

'I never forget a face' is a common phrase – often said by people who can't remember names very well! How much do you really notice about a new acquaintance? Learning to observe faces accurately and in detail stimulates the imagination and will help you to put names to faces more accurately.

It is common to make a quick assessment as to whether we find someone attractive to look at or not, but that on its own does not help us to remember a name. We tend to look closely at the eyes and the mouth when we speak or listen to people; but how much do we actually see? It is more useful to notice key features, in an objective way, to use as triggers for your imagination and memory associations. Look for the following:

The eyes

Look at the size of the eyes.

- *Are they: Large? Small? Protruding? Deep-set? Close together? Far apart?*

Look at the colour of the eyes.

- *Are they: Blue? Grey? Green? Brown? Hazel? Black? Flecked?*

Look at the area around the eyes.

○ *Is the skin: Puffy? Smooth? Wrinkled? Firm?*

The mouth

Look at the lips.

○ *Are they: Thin? Full? Upturned? Downturned? Well-shaped? Even? Uneven?*

The head

Look at the size of the head.

○ *Is it: Large? Medium? Small?*

Look at the shape of the head.

○ *Is it: Square? Rectangular? Round/Oval? Triangular?*

Look at the bone structure.

○ *Is it: Broad? Narrow? Big-boned? Fine-boned?*

Look at the side of the head.

○ *Does the shape appear noticeably different from the side than from the front?*

Hair

Look at the texture and colour of the hair.

○ *Is it: Long? Short? Grey? Highlighted? Wavy? Straight? Thick? Fine? Cropped? Shaved?*

Forehead

Look at the forehead and the space between the hairline and the eyebrows.

○ *Is it: High? Wide? Narrow between hairline and eyebrows? Narrow between the temples? Smooth? Lined?*

Look at the eyebrows.

○ *Are they: Thick? Thin? Long? Short? Arched? Close together? Far apart? Flat? Plucked? Bushy? Tapered?*

Ears

Ears are a part of the face that often go unremarked upon, and yet they are one of our most distinguishing features.

○ *Are they: Large? Small? Flat against the head? Protruding? Smooth-lobed? Wrinkled? Small-lobed? Large-lobed? Pierced?*

Nose

A person's nose can often seem to dominate the head and it is one physical feature about which most of us have an opinion. Look at the nose from the front and the side.

○ *Is it: Large? Small? Narrow? Wide? Crooked? Straight? Pointed? Upturned? Bulbous?*

○ *Are the nostrils: Wide? Narrow? Flared? Hairy? Curved down or up?*

Then look in the same way at other physical features, such as the skin, chin, cheekbones, eyelashes and hands. (Of course, you will need to make all these observations in a very natural way.)

Use your other senses to recall scent, voice, mood, conversation: anything that will help you to make an association between name and person. Sometimes comparing one person with another can also help to remind you of their distinctive features.

Suzie Rose might be confused with *Susan Flower,* but one can be separated from the other if Suzie is remembered as being petite in height (and having a shorter name) and wearing floral (rose) scent; whereas Susan is tall and full-figured with 'big' hair, like a flower in full bloom.

Mike *McGuinness* can be remembered by his white 'frothy' moustache and smooth demeanour (rather like the drink of the same name); whereas Jim *Maclaren* has a long, lean chin (reminiscent of the smooth-bodied racing car).

Common names and suggestions for memory association

You may want to alter these and add to them to suit your own imagination and associations:

White The white cliffs of Dover.

Brown A freshly-ploughed field.

Green An enormous green tree.

Smith A smithy with an anvil and hammer.

Collins A large collie dog going into an inn. (Collie + inns.)

More unusual names can be remembered by breaking them down into syllables that have associations. The more absurd the image in your mind, the more likely you are to remember the name:

MacIntyre A large hamburger in a large tyre.

Abado The Swedish pop group at a party. (Abba + 'do'.)

Charalambous Two people sitting on the back of a large lamb at a bus stop. (Share a lamb + bus.)

Of course, you can always apply this principle to first names as well.

In conclusion

The more frequently you use this technique as a mental 'aide mémoire' the quicker the habit will form and the more easily you will come up with associations and imaginative references that work well for you. For those of you who are musical, transforming the rhythmic sound of an unusual first name into a tune may help; or you can experiment with combining the Name–Face technique with other skills in your memory repertoire.

As with all the other techniques in this book, the key to recall is choosing a reliable memory trigger. Whatever your approach, remember that including colour, movement, exaggeration and sensual references will stimulate your imagination, and including an element of familiar reality will ground your creativity in a rock-solid association.

In no time at all you will be able to remember the names of people you meet – which will have positive benefits for your social and business life, and will naturally boost your confidence.

6 TEST YOUR MEMORY

Before you embark on these tests, you may find it useful to look back at the guidelines on page 38 to remind yourself of effective ways to create and connect Key Images and to stimulate your whole brain.

1 The Link Story Test

Read through the following list of ten items, once only.

Using the Link Story System described on pages 42–4, use Key Images to memorize all of the items as well as the order in which they are listed.

Turn to page 84 to test yourself, and for scoring instructions.

Newspaper	**Knife**
River	**Hammer**
Trousers	**Clock**
Wool	**Doctor**
Yoghurt	**Tree**

2 The Number–Shape Test

Using the Number–Shape System (see pages 48–54), review the list of ten words below. Your aim is to remember each item by *pegging* it to the appropriate number shape.

Turn to page 84 to test yourself, and for scoring instructions.

1 Symphony	**2 Prayer**	**3 Melon**
4 Volcano	**5 Bicycle**	**6 Sunshine**
7 Apple pie	**8 Blossom**	**9 Spaceship**
10 Field of wheat		

3 The Number–Rhyme Test

Using the Number–Rhyme System explained on pages 54–60, give yourself one minute to memorize the following list of ten items. The aim is to remember each item by *pegging* it to the appropriate Number–Rhyme Key Image using as many of the Memory Principles from pages 30–8 as possible.

Turn to page 85 to test yourself, and for scoring instructions.

1 Planet	**2 Daisy**	**3 Microphone**
4 Armchair	**5 Road**	**6 Wallpaper**
7 Sports car	**8 Ketchup**	**9 Toothbrush**	**10 Soap**

4 The Alphabet Test

The following questions will encourage you to remember the general rules and guidelines that apply to the Alphabet System described on pages 61–3. Turn to page 86 to fill in your answers.

Which of the following words are the ideal choices for representing the following letters, and why:

1 The letter K: cake   kerb

2 The letter B: bee   bar

3 The letter C: crease   see

4 The letter F: fee   effervescence

5 Draw the Key Image that was recommended to represent the letter 'I'.

5 The Memory Room Test

Using the Memory Room System described on pages 64–6, give yourself one minute to study the picture below. Then turn to page 86 and list as many items as you can remember next to their relevant location in the room. Remember that the order of the items and imaginative detail are of prime importance.

6 The Name–Face Test

Give yourself one minute to study these names and faces, using the Face–Name System (see pages 67–78). The aim is to create associations between the person's name and any distinguishing visual characteristics, in order to create memorable connections. Turn to page 87 to answer the questions.

1 Mr Hawkins

2 Mrs Swanson

3 Mr Fisher

4 Mr Ramm

5 Miss Temple

Results and Summary
1 Link Story test response
Relate your Link Story to yourself or out loud and write down your list of twenty Key Word items, in their correct order, here.

_____

_____

_____

_____

_____

_____

_____

_____

Score yourself in two ways:

How many did you remember correctly?

How many were in the correct order?

Score one point for each item remembered correctly.

Score one point for each item remembered in the correct order.

Total score possible: 40

2 Number–Shape test response
Write down the item you have memorized for each of the following numbers. Write them down in the order indicated:

9 _____

2 _____

8 _____

7 _____

6 _____

3 _____

5 _____

10	
1	
4	

Score one point for each item you have next to the correct number.
Total score possible: 10

3 Number–Rhyme test response

Write down each item you have memorized, next to the word
for the Number–Rhyme image that you pegged it to. Write them
down in the order indicated:

Number Rhyme peg	Item from list on page 81
9	
2	
8	
6	
7	
3	
5	
4	
1	
10	

Score one point for each item you have next to the correct number.
Total score possible: 10

4 The Alphabet System test response

Write your answers to the questions on page 81 here, bearing in mind that the Alphabet System described on pages 61–3 is based on sounds. The answers can be found on page 88.

1 _____

2 _____

3 _____

4 _____

5 _____

Score two points for each correct answer and explanation.
Total score possible: 10

5 The Memory Room test response

Imagine yourself walking around the memory room and recall each location and the associated items in order. List as many as you can remember here. Then check your answers against the illustration on page 82.

Location (target number of items)	List of items
Floor (5 items)	
Table (4 items)	
Sofa (3 items)	
Pillars (2 items)	
Statue (1 item)	

Score one point for each correct item.
Target score: 15

6 Name–Face test response

Using the Name–Face System described on pages 67–78, use visual associations and your imagination to recall the correct name for each face.

Try to write them down in the order below:

5 _____

4 _____

1 _____

2 _____

3 _____

Score one point for each face that you name correctly.
Total score possible: 5

Answers to the Alphabet Test

Correct answers are as follows (see pages 61–3 for a reminder of the reasons why).

1 The word that could be used to represent the letter 'K' is cake because it begins with the sound of the letter 'K'.

2 The ideal word to represent the letter 'B' is bee, because it spells the letter, and sounds like the letter, as well as starting with the letter.

3 The best word to represent the letter 'C' is the word see, because it spells the letter and sounds like the letter.

4 The word to represent the letter 'F' is the word effort because it begins with the sound of the letter 'F'.

5 The Key Image recommended to represent the letter 'I' is a picture of an eye, because the word sounds like the letter and is easy to remember.

Test result summary

The tests in this chapter are designed to help you to see the progress you are making as you practise the various memory techniques and become familiar with the Link, Peg and other systems.

The formula below explains how you can calculate your overall score as a percentage of the total possible result.

Test	Your Score	Possible Score
The Link Story Test		40
The Number–Shape Test		10
The Number–Rhyme Test		10
The Alphabet Test		10
The Memory Room Test		15
The Name–Face Test		5
Total score		90

To calculate your total score as a percentage of the possible total score follow these guidelines:

First, divide the *Total Possible Score* (**90**) by the total of *Your Score* (**YS**)
90/YS = *Your Result*

Then, divide **100** by *Your Result* (**YR**).
○ 100/YR = *Your Result* as an overall percentage of the *Total Possible Score*

For example:
If *Your Score* = 40, you would calculate as follows:
90/40 = 22.5 (*Your Result*)
100/22.5 = 40% (*Your Result* as a percentage of the *Total Possible Score*)

Normal scores on each of these tests range from 20 to 60 per cent. Once you have mastered the techniques in this book, you can expect to achieve scores between 90 and 100 per cent every time.

Remember – whichever memory system you choose to use, make sure that you make the images and associations positive and fun for your memory to recall!

7   DOUBLE YOUR MEMORY POWER

The ice factor

Now in one magical moment you can increase by 100 per cent everything that you have learned so far!

> O You have learned up to six Memory Systems that can be applied to almost all circumstances where you need to remember core information.
>
> O You have chosen your Key Words and transformed them into images.
>
> O You have used your imagination and created associations that will help your memory to recall effectively.
>
> O You have practised using them to a point where you enjoy the images and they are second nature to you.
>
> O You feel comfortable that you can rely upon them to be your key memory triggers, recalling information on demand, from your memory.

If that is the case, then the time has come to *freeze* them in your memory. This will have the benefit of *immediately doubling* your memory power.

Review each of the systems in turn:

◉ Imagine the first of your Key Words and focus on its Key Image.

◉ Be certain that you know what its Key Image looks like, sounds like, feels like, tastes like; how it moves, how it exists in space, and how you use it.

◉ Now imagine that Key Image embedded in a huge block of ice.